JOBS

By Joanna Brundle

A Look at Life Around the World

60000508726

BookLife
PUBLISHING

©This edition was published in 2022. First published in 2019.

BookLife Publishing Ltd.
King's Lynn, Norfolk
PE30 4LS, UK

ISBN: 978-1-80155-571-5

Written by:
Joanna Brundle

Edited by:
Kirsty Holmes

Designed by:
Jasmine Pointer

A catalogue record for this book is available from the British Library.

CONTENTS

Page 4   All Kinds of Jobs

Page 6   Working with Animals

Page 8   Working with Food

Page 10   Jobs in Transport

Page 12   Jobs in Tourism and Leisure

Page 14   Working Children

Page 16   Jobs in Healthcare

Page 18   Working in the Emergency Services

Page 20   Jobs in Sport

Page 22   A Job in Space

Page 23   Glossary

Page 24   Index

Words that look like <u>this</u> can be found in the glossary on page 23.

ALL KINDS OF JOBS

Every day, millions of people go to work. They might work inside or outside, alone or in a team, travelling or at home. In this book, we shall take a trip around the world to find out about the different jobs that they do.

What jobs do you think these people do?

WHY DO PEOPLE HAVE JOBS?

People work to earn money. They use the money to look after their families and buy things they need. At work, people may help others, be creative or learn new skills.

WORKING WITH ANIMALS

All around the world, people work as vets, in zoos, in sea life centres or wildlife sanctuaries. Some look after dogs or horses. Others work on <u>conservation</u> projects, protecting animals in danger. Some work on farms.

A zookeeper in Israel gets a friendly lick from a giraffe.

ANIMAL HELPERS

China, India and Australia are important sheep-producing countries. Shepherds use dogs to help them round up the sheep.

Shepherd, UK

The US produces more cattle than any other country. Cowboys use horses and a rope called a lasso to round up the animals.

Cowboys in South American countries are called gauchos.

Farmer, US

7

WORKING WITH FOOD

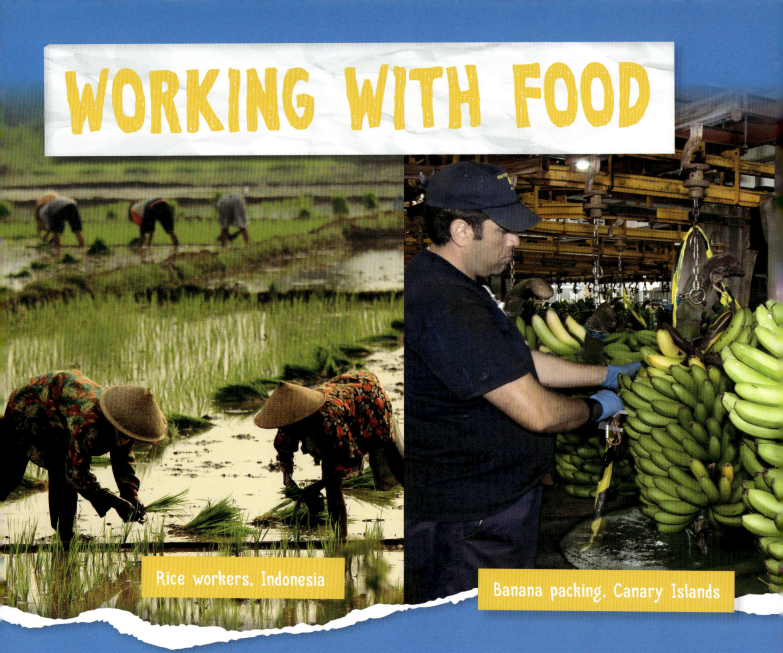

Rice workers, Indonesia

Banana packing, Canary Islands

People grow, pack, transport, prepare and cook food. A large amount of the world's population work growing crops or raising animals for food. People also work in markets, shops, supermarkets and restaurants, selling and serving food.

Do you like chocolate? Let's see what sort of jobs people do to make it.

1

Cocoa bean picking, Indonesia

2

Chocolate factory, Belgium

3

Chocolate shop, France

It takes a lot of different people doing lots of different jobs to make and sell chocolate.

JOBS IN TRANSPORT

Rickshaw taxi, India

Moving people and goods creates lots of jobs on trains, buses, taxis, ships and ferries.

A rickshaw is also known as a tuk-tuk because of the noise it makes.

Air travel provides jobs for pilots and <u>air traffic controllers</u>. Airports also <u>employ</u> workers in shops, cafes and restaurants.

Heathrow Airport, UK

Some places have very famous forms of transport. New York City, US is famous for its yellow taxis and their drivers. London is famous for its black cabs. London cab drivers have to pass a special test called The Knowledge to prove they know their way around.

Yellow taxis, New York

Gondoliers make their living working on the canals of Venice, Italy.

JOBS IN TOURISM AND LEISURE

A London beefeater

Beefeaters work as tour guides at the world-famous Tower of London.

Travelling to new places is called tourism. Many people work in tourism, looking after the needs of travellers. They work in hotels, restaurants and tourist attractions, such as theme parks. Some work as tour guides, showing tourists around.

In cold countries, people work as ski and snowboard instructors. Some work in mountain rescue teams that help people trapped in heavy snow. In sunny countries like Australia, people find work as beach lifeguards.

Lifeguard, Manly Beach, Sydney, Australia

A ski instructor with his pupils in the Alps in Germany

WORKING CHILDREN

This boy is collecting plastic bottles on a rubbish dump in India.

This boy earns money by selling the bottles for <u>recycling</u>.

Some children do not get the chance to go to school or to play. They have to go to work from an early age. They earn money to help their families. Around the world, about 200 million children work instead of going to school.

This little girl is harvesting corn in Thailand.

This boy is working in a brick factory.

Most child workers are employed on farms. The farms grow crops like coffee, cotton and rubber. Some child workers are employed in factories. They make clothes, carpets, toys, matches and cigarettes. Child workers work long hours, earn very little and their work is often dangerous.

JOBS IN HEALTHCARE

Some healthcare workers work in clean, modern hospitals. Others work without proper equipment and medicines. Volunteers work in places where people have been injured in wars or <u>natural disasters</u>.

These doctors are helping survivors of an earthquake.

People living in <u>rural</u> areas of Australia may have to travel long distances to visit the hospital. The Royal Flying Doctor Service flies doctors directly to these patients. This means people can see a doctor if there is an emergency.

Flying Doctors, Australia

WORKING IN THE EMERGENCY SERVICES

The emergency services include the police, the fire brigade and ambulance services. Trained people work for these services all around the world.

These firefighters in Australia are trying to bring a <u>wildfire</u> under control.

Police Officers, Italy

The RCMP is the police force of Canada. It was set up in 1920 and officers originally rode horses. Horses are still used for special events, including the Musical Ride. Officers and their horses take part in performances that raise money for charity.

Officers in the RCMP are called 'Mounties'.

The bright red uniforms of the RCMP are recognised all over the world.

JOBS IN SPORT

Wembley Stadium, UK

Over 5,000 people work at Wembley on match days.

People who play sports for a job are called athletes. Sport also provides jobs in television, and for <u>coaches</u>, umpires and people working at sports arenas. Television companies employ sports reporters, <u>commentators</u> and presenters, and stream live sport all around the world.

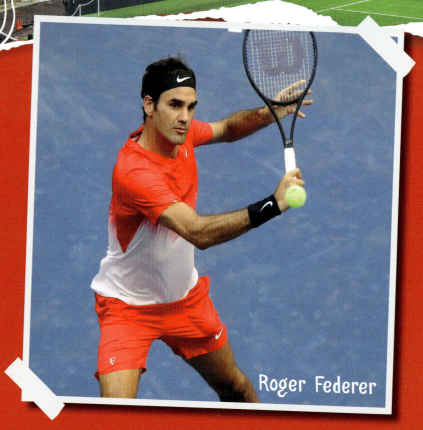

Roger Federer

Football is played <u>professionally</u> in almost every country in the world.

Formula One drivers are employed to race all over the world, from Australia to Russia, Italy to China. A team of people including mechanics, medical staff and chefs travel with them.

A team of mechanics working on a car during a race in Malaysia.

A JOB IN SPACE

Some people do a job that is out of this world! Up to six astronauts work on the ISS – the International Space Station. This is a large spacecraft that <u>orbits</u> the Earth in space. Astronauts work in space for about six months.

The ISS

Most of the ISS astronauts have come from the US and Russia.

GLOSSARY

air traffic controllers	people who direct aircraft on the ground and in the air to prevent accidents
coaches	people whose job is to teach and train a sports team or sports person
commentators	someone who describes what is happening at a sporting event
conservation	the protection of things found in nature
employ	to give someone a job
natural disasters	natural events that cause great damage to an area and its people
orbits	travels around a star or planet in space in a regular path
professionally	when someone does something as their job
recycling	reusing materials for different purposes
rural	relating to the countryside
wildfire	a fire in a wild area such as a forest that burns fiercely and out of control

INDEX

agriculture 6–9, 15

airports 10

animals 6–8, 19

children 14–15

emergency services 16–19

factories 9, 15

healthcare 16–18

hospitals 16–17

money 5, 14, 19

restaurants 8, 10, 12

shops 8–10

space 22

sport 20–21

tourism 12–13

transport 8, 10–11

Photocredits: Abbreviations: l–left, r–right, b–bottom, t–top, c–centre, m–middle.
All images are courtesy of Shutterstock.com. With thanks to Getty Images, Thinkstock Photo and iStockphoto.

Front cover – Tukaram.Karve, wavebreakmedia, Monkey Business Images. 2 – Ververidis Vasilis. 4 – Rawpixel.com. 5 – iMoved Studio. 6 – Roman Yanushevsky. 7t – Shaun Barr. 7b – CLP Media. 8l – thomaschristiawan. 8r – Salvador Aznar. 9t – INDONESIAPIX. 9bl – photo-denver. 9br – P-Kheawtasang. 10t – Dmitry Kalinovsky. 10b – Ondrej Zabransky. 11t – Bufflerump. 11b – kavalenkava. 12 – chrisdorney. 13l – Julia Kuznetsova. 13r – katacarix. 14 – clicksabhi. 15m – Zvonimir AtleticT. 15tr – SOMRERK WITTHAYANANT. 16 – Worldpics. 17 – VanderWolf Images. 18l – Mari_May. 18r – Marco Aprile. 19 – Darlene Munro. 20t – Yuri Turkov. 20b – Leonard Zhukovsky. 21t – Jefferson Bernardes. 21b– Abdul Razak Latif. 22 – 3Dsculptor.